THE TRUMPET SOUNDS

by

Robert Lee Byrd
with
Doris Ann Hartley Byrd

The Brethren Press, Elgin, Illinois

THE TRUMPET SOUNDS

Copyright © 1981, by Doris Ann Hartley Byrd

Cover Design by Marjorie Vandruff

Library of Congress Cataloging in Publication Data

Byrd, Robert Lee, 1898-1975.
  The trumpet sounds.

  1. Byrd, Robert Lee, 1898-1975. 2. Church of the Brethren—Clergy—Biography. 3. Clergy—United States—Biography. 4. Byrd, Doris Ann Hartley, 1904-
I. Byrd, Doris Ann Hartley, 1904-   joint author. II. Title.
BX7843.B93A37   286'.5 [B]   80-29196
ISBN 0-87178-878-0

Published by The Brethren Press, Elgin, Illinois 60120

Printed in the United States of America

Dedicated to

Our son, Ernest,
Our grandsons, Richard and Robert,
Our great-grandsons, Marc and Michael

Acknowledgments

I am deeply grateful to the following, Nancy Vickers for transcribing from the tapes, Virginia Andes for reading the manuscript and making helpful suggestions, Robert Sherfy for encouragement and for writing the foreword, Janet Earhart for the final typing of the manuscript, the host of fellow travelers along the way, and to the Brethren Press for making it possible to share Robert's story with you.

Doris Ann Hartley Byrd

Contents

Foreword, by Robert L. Sherfy   7

Introduction   9

Part One
  Measured for Decay   13
  School on Windy Ridge   16
  Logs and Bees   19
  Poisoned   22

Part Two
  A Year of Mysterious Events   25
  Spelling Each Other Down   27
  A Good Rattlesnake Dog   30
  The Good Old Days   32
  A Happy Time Singing Together   34
  "Preacher"   37
  The Daily Roundup   40
  My Dog, Sport   42
  We Become Lumberjacks   44
  Serving Death Notices to Bees   47
Part Three
  My Little Sister   51
  A Big Step   53

Wedding Bells	56
A New Life	60
"The Model T"	62
A Seven Day Nightmare	64

Part Four

A Second Chance	69
Another Move	71
A Higher Goal	73
College and More	76
We Live in a Tent	79
The Great Achievement	83

Part Five

At the Sound of a Trumpet	85
The Executive Mansion	89
A Sharing Friend	91
Our Son, Ernest	93

Part Six

North of the Border?	97
A New Country	99
Welcomed Through the Portals	102
Mountain Miracles	105
Country Hospitality	108
A Baptistry Healing	113
Six Wedding Rings	116
Home Sweet Home	118
Preparing the Way	121
The Last Move	124
Sunset Days	125

Foreword

I've known Robert and Doris Byrd since that day in the fall of 1929 when they and their belongings arrived on a Model T truck at Daleville Academy. Their combination of commitment, talent and courage both amazed and inspired me many times during those years.

Doris knows his story well; she shared most of it as his fine, faithful partner. She reports it in a direct, appealing way.

Robert was a minister in the Church of the Brethren for nearly 54 years. He was my classmate at both Daleville Academy and Bridgewater College. Years later, when he had retired from pastoral work, I was privileged to be his pastor. During that time we were often together and had time to talk about our lives and their value. When he was young, Robert's dedication to his "calling" impressed me. I was even more impressed by his faithfulness to it, through thick and thin, until death.

I personally have not known anyone whose life included as wide a variety of difficult and discouraging circumstances *and* as consistent a pattern of usefulness to the church in a variety of situations.

I think Oscar Blackwelder's quote applies to

Robert Byrd:

"Great it is to believe the dream
When you stand in youth by the starlit stream;
But a greater thing is to see life through,
And to say at the end, 'The dream was true'."

Robert L. Sherfy
Mount Solon, Va.

Introduction

The story you are about to read is a true story of a courageous man, his experiences and struggles from birth to the end of his life.

Robert had been urged to write and share with a wider public some of the things he often used as illustrations in his teaching and preaching during his ministry.

During the last year of his life he recorded some of the highlights of his life on tape. He did not begin until in August of 1974 when he was very ill, and concluded in October. I think he had in mind to go back over what he had recorded as the most vivid incidents in his life and fill in with more detail. This was not to be. He grew constantly worse, with multiple-myeloma bone cancer and died a few months after the end of this taping.

I did not know what he had recorded until a year later, when I could bring myself to play the tapes. I also think his story should be shared with his friends and the public. This has been a very emotional experience for me, as I shared the life he talks about for almost 54 years. The earlier years of his life I learned about by going over most of the road he had traveled, and meeting many of the people he talked about.

I want this to be his story, so I have only edited it to the extent that there would not be too many overlaps in the story as it was taken from the tapes, since he recorded it a little at a time over a period of several weeks.

Robert was a very fluent speaker and an excellent student of literature. I am sure had he been setting this story down on paper he would have written it in a much different and more correct style. Any mistakes will be ours, not his. I share with you his story as it is, hoping you will enjoy and perhaps profit by it as much as I have. Even though, I was there for most of the time, I too can appreciate and enjoy even more by reading it than when it was "happening" to us.

Robert was very modest and did not lay any claim to fame or accomplishments. So many things went unnoticed and not credited to him in his lifetime. He was always too busy with the work at hand to do much about keeping records.

He speaks of the music and instruments he played in his younger days, along with friends of that time. He had an almost perfect-pitch for music of any kind. When he came in contact with the more sacred hymns and sophisticated music, he became a great lover of classical music and had a large collection of the works of many of the great composers. He always worked toward improving the music and musical instruments in all the churches he served.

At the dedication of the Junior Church, West Virginia, in 1940, Russell West had just ended the first revival services in the new church. It was at this time Robert picked up the art of playing the "saw" from Russell, who was not only an evangelist, but an artist as well. He painted the large waterfall picture behind the baptistry, and also played the "saw." At first Robert just used one of the handsaws that had been left from building the church, making his first bow from hairs from a "horse's tail," later purchasing a violin bow.

Many called it the "musical saw," however, it was just a plain Atkins handsaw purchased at the Kayne and Keyser Hardware Store in Belington, W. Va. The music from the saw has a tone much like the violin. He was much in demand wherever we lived to render special numbers. In the churches he served as pastor or in an evangelistic meeting the saw was always near by, and he would pick it up and accompany the music being played. He was often referred to as the "preacher with the musical saw."

He was a great Bible student, having memorized many portions of Scripture, until he could quote entire chapters. If he was called on to preach or teach on short notice, it made no difference. Even without notes he could deliver a discourse. He did not write out his sermons, but made a rough outline, filling in as he went along. I have listened to the same sermon topic dozens of times, but never found it boring as the content was always new and inspiring. He was never so happy as when he was teaching or preaching.

Robert was a visiting pastor, and also a builder of churches. I do not recall a single church in which he served where there was not new facilities built, finishing up ones that had been started, or some type of renovation done or plans set in motion for needed additions. He cooperated fully in interdenominational efforts and was a firm believer in the larger fellowship of the church. He was also a poet, having written hundreds of poems many of which have been published in various magazines and papers. A few are included in this book.

Now may I leave you with Robert Lee Byrd, my husband, as he tells the story of his life. You will find him in many unique situations, dangerous and exciting, as well as interesting and without a doubt challenging.

> Doris Ann Hartley Byrd
> Bridgewater, Virginia

PART ONE

Measured for Decay

This recording is begun in August 1974, for the purpose of recording a sort of autobiography or story of my life. It is a strange story, so strange that few will believe it, few will be interested in listening to it and those who do might discredit it because of its unreasonable content.

It is recorded for the purpose of my satisfaction as I sit alone, and it might be interesting to my grandsons or perhaps some of my friends. It may be of interest and helpful also to record for a larger audience the struggles of a mountain boy, and the strange incidents and adventures through which he went in a short lifetime.

I hardly know where to begin, except to say that as far as the calendar is concerned and as recorded in the court house of Buckhannon, West Virginia, I was born February 27, 1898, midway between three biblical hamlets—Goshen, Canaan and Eden—in a log cabin at the foot of a mountain. My parents' names were George Robert Byrd and Georganna Sophia Ware Byrd. My mother was never proud of her middle name, Sophia. Why, I do not know. I never heard her use it nor ever admit it, although I never saw or heard anything wrong about it. It was a good name as names go, for all names are good or bad as we make them.

At the time of my arrival on this celestial planet there was no doctor in attendance; there was only a midwife, a lady by the name of Roby, as I was told later. She was a skillful midwife, seldom losing a case. She knew nothing of medicine or medical practice but knew a great deal about herbs and herbalistic treatments that usually brought the infant and mother through safely, and she was always proud of her achievements.

When I was nine days old according to her custom I was measured for the "decay." Don't ask me to explain to you what that is; I can only describe it as an imaginary something that was treated with an egg and a yarn string before an open fireplace. The yarn, after it was cast through, was wrapped around the egg, then unwrapped and made into a loop, and the child was passed through the loop nine times. The loop was then wrapped around the egg again and the egg was laid upon the hearth before a open hot fire. If the child was a healthy child nothing happened, but if the child had "decay" the yarn would burn off, which meant that further treatment of some sort had to be administered in order to bring that child up to normal. How it culminated in my case I do not know, but it was sufficient to last for 76 years at least.

School on Windy Ridge

My educational career began in 1906 on Windy Ridge, three miles from Hacker Valley, W. Va., in Webster County. My first two schools were taught by German teachers and were of various durations. The first one in 1906 was taught by Annie Merckley, a maiden lady. I have dated cards that she gave me as Awards of Merit and that's how I remember. It was a good school of only three months. The winter was very severe it seemed to me then, and my father would put me on his shoulders and carry me for the distance to the schoolhouse, then return for me in the evening. Once you entered the schoolhouse and the bell had rung, there was as near absolute silence as can be imagined in a school room. It was a one room building that seated about 35 to 40 students and was always full. No whispering was allowed and time was given strictly to study and recitation. It was a very exacting process.

I well remember how that we were required to stand up before the entire school and recite and the class which sat on the recitation bench was supposed to be our critics. If in reading we made a single mistake in enunciation, pronunciation or deletion we were stopped immediately and corrected. That was the instruction and that followed throughout the first schools I attended.

The second school was taught by Martha Balley, and was of six months duration. The settlement in which we lived was Swiss-German and I heard the Swiss-German language spoken most of the time, but this was not used in recitation or in conversation between us students. I can well remember the names of those predominately outstanding students who were there; not only the Balleys, the Gobleys and the Woodricks but many other German names. Even though it was an exacting school I was reluctant to leave when school closed after the second year. My father moved into a lumber camp and I did not get to go to school anymore for quite some time. But be it said that I had learned to read; in fact, it seems to me that I could read a little before beginning school in 1906. I had learned to read from Mother's Bible. I have that Bible yet in my library still kept in the original box in which it came. It was presented to her and Father in 1900 by her Uncle Sam Grimes, after a fire had destroyed their home and all its contents, and almost me. It was in large print and contained only the New Testament, but I spent much time in reading it and I delighted in it especially when there was a thunderstorm in progress, for in those days I was fearful of thunderstorms. I am not anymore. I really enjoy thunderstorms; they are music to me and I have recorded thunderstorms many times on my tape recorder and enjoy listening to them over and over again. But in my younger days the harder it thundered the more deeply I snuggled down in my bed and sometimes hid my head under the pillow until the storm would pass over. I had learned and committed to memory many passages of the scriptures by the time I had entered into other grades of school.

Logs and Bees

For a period of time now I was at home with my father and mother who worked in the lumber camp. Father stacked lumber, and Mother cooked for the mill crews and the woods crews, a considerable number of men. We lived in a little house that had been constructed especially for us, "shacks" they were called then. I had no boyfriends to play with and at the age of ten I wandered up and down the tramway all alone seeking entertainment wherever I could find it. I can well remember the most interesting thing that I found to do was fishing for brook trout. I had several holes along Laurel Fork in which there were almost always some nice brook trout. All I needed to do was bait my hook, slip up unseen, drop the hook over a log into the water, and almost immediately I had myself one of the nicest brook trout you ever did see. That was one of my chief joys during that period of time.

Other times I wandered up and down the tramways looking for something to do. I spent a great deal of time around the saw mill washing logs. The logs were dirty, sandy, muddy and had to be cleaned before running them through the saw. Why they did it I do not know, but they permitted me to stand on the skidway with a hose, hot water running through the hose, and wash the logs. More than once I was pulled out from beneath rolling logs and saved by somebody who was near at hand, which some providence seemed to have placed there especially to do the job. I was afraid of the mill and yet it had a strange attraction to me, the noise of the mill scared me and yet I could not stay away from it.

One day the cutting crew, those who cut the trees, found a bee tree. They came into the camp and got a new washtub, took it out to the tree and brought back nearly a full tub of the most beautiful amber honey I have ever seen.

They said they didn't get it all, so the following day a young boy who had just come into the camp to visit his parents for a few days and I decided that we would go out and finish the job. We got ourselves a couple of buckets, some rags, sticks, and knives, an ax and some matches, and took off to the woods to the bee tree. There we intended to gather the honey that had been left behind by the men.

We lit our torches and got everything ready to gather honey. We were getting along quite well and it seemed to me we had a lot of honey in our buckets, when all at once one of my torches burst into flames. The torches were used to just smoke the bees so they couldn't sting, not burn them. That was the last of our honey gathering. The fire consumed what was left of the honey, while we hurried back to camp with what we had gathered. The tree, as I remember it, was so dry that it burned into ashes the complete length of the tree.

Poisoned

It was during this spell in the woods where my parents worked for the saw mill that I became violently ill. I had eaten some canned corn, which I dearly loved, that had become contaminated. I had contracted ptomaine poisoning, food poison, or as some called it then, "canker" poisoning. I was really ill. They called for a doctor from 20 miles away, who had to come part way by railway and the balance of the way by incline. If you don't know what an incline is let me explain: it was a truck suspended on the end of a cable which was wrapped around a large drum at the top of the mountain. There it was operated by machinery which would pull the truck, loaded or empty, up the side of the hill, drop it down the other side, unload it or load it whichever the case might be, and send it back up and over again. That went on throughout the day. The doctor came across the mountain in this manner and proceeded immediately to administer the only remedy that he knew. He gave me Calomel, which is an extract of Calomelas that grew in the swamps. It is a very nauseating sort of herb tea. The Calomelas plant resembles a flag and would make you deathly sick if you ate it outright, for it is a poison. But it was supposed to be also the only thing that could purify, that would empty the stomach and purify the blood, so the doctor gave me a strong course of Calomel accompanied with castor oil and epsom salts.

Why it didn't kill me I'll never know, unless a higher power had a job for me to do later in life. I was so violently ill I had become delirious and no one thought I would live. I suppose that today under the same circumstances, I would have been considered hopeless, but after a period of eight to ten days I began to recover, and after many weeks to gain my old strength back. But I never again liked corn very well, nor the medicine I was given, if it could have been called medicine. And I shall never forget Dr. Francis Austin Fisher who came to my aid up the river and over the mountains.

PART TWO

A Year of Mysterious Events

So we come to the end of a very important period in my life. In fact, it marks a very important change in almost every respect. The Urban Lumber Company completed their contract of cutting the tract of timber they had bought, sold their sawmill and moved away, leaving behind a desolate, mutilated forest and many men without work. It became necessary, therefore, for my father to move and look for another job. Jobs were very difficult to find in those days. In fact, a job was almost like looking for the traditional needle in a haystack. We went over into Upshur County and purchased a small tract of land, consisting of about 37 acres, and built a home.

I well remember that year for it is marked by some very important events. That was the year, 1910, when Halley's Comet became visible, and I saw it repeatedly night after night for a considerable period of time as it swooped across the heavens with its long tail trailing behind it. That was the year when I saw what looked like the moon falling from the heavens. That was the year when I saw a great ball of fire, bright as the sun, sweeping through the sky across the meadow. It was not a bolt of lightning; it struck nothing; it was just a phenomenon that I never could explain.

That was the year of one of the impossibles that I could not explain and that you will not believe happened to me. I saw floating in the heavens among the storm clouds the most beautiful woman I had ever seen in all of my life. She floated along the clouds ever so far and then, folding her arms, she looked down at me and smiled sweetly and toppled over out of sight in the clouds. These are some of the events that make me remember that year very vividly, and which I shall never forget.

We completed building the house, moved in it and started clearing the land for the next year's crop. It had been cleared before, quite a number of years before, and was not as difficult to clear now as it would have been formerly. In that country there were tremendous forests, virgin forests we might call them, with the most beautiful and giant trees that I have seen anywhere before or since. These have long since disappeared from the landscape due to the greed of the lumber companies. They came in and slaughtered the landscape for the lumber that was to be had.

part of our instruction, in almost drill-like fashion in my early school days. Those instructions have always stayed with me.

A Good Rattlesnake Dog

Those were the days, as I look back across the years, that must be classed as the happiest days of my life, though at the time I knew it not. Those were the days of having few companions or boyfriends. I wandered over the hills and fields with my muzzle loading rifle over my shoulder, with my little dog at my heels, hunting in the woods, looking for ginseng, just having a good time.

Those were the days that I hunted Daniel Boone style or Kit Carson and Davy Crockett style. I had a rifle, a 32-caliber long-barrel bore, and I had practiced enough so I could take the head off a squirrel at quite a distance almost every shot. I had a dog that was the most marvelous dog I ever owned. He was a squirrel dog and he knew how to handle the situation. He was also a good rattlesnake dog. He hated rattlesnakes and when he bayed a certain tone I knew it was a rattlesnake. When I would reach the scene of his baying I would find him going about in a wide circle, and between us we'd finish off the snake. He was certainly a marvelous companion in the woods. He was a good watch dog and had intelligence far beyond what one could have believed a dog could ordinarily possess.

There were days that I wandered through the woods and learned the identity of as many things as I could. I knew many trees by name. I learned to know all of the trees that grew in my vicinity. I could even go to them at night and feel them and tell what they were, recognizing them from the kind of bark.

I learned to know many of the weeds and although my parents had very little botanical education, they and the neighbors taught me the names of a great many herbs and weeds. Later when I got into school and into the study of botany I discovered that strangely enough they were almost all correct. They had taught me well. Those were happy days of my life although there were hard days and difficult situations to live through, as there still are in many sections of the country where I lived as a boy. They were marvelous days to live over again as I look back across the many, many years.

The Good Old Days

Those were the days when those who got a job worked. Today work seemingly is done largely by "standing" armies. I know of a building that is being constructed by what seems to be a standing committee. Several men will stand around watching one or maybe two work. If you will go around where construction work is in progress, it might be you will discover the same is true wherever you go. We worked long hard hours in those days, and if the boss found you taking time out, what nowadays would be considered a coffee or cigarette break, or just a rest break, you lost your job. My boss, when I worked as a logger in the woods or other public-work jobs, watched his men or even spied on them as he went around in the woods or wherever they worked. If he found them sitting down on the job, when they came in at noon or in the evening he had their time cards figured and their money ready for them and they were sent home, no longer employed.

They were ten-hour days, which started after we had a big breakfast. They had good cooks in the kitchen and we ate good meals of well prepared food before we went to work. We were supposed to be at work by 7:00 a.m. We worked until

12 noon, then the boss in a loud husky voice would call time for dinner. The dinner or noon meal, consisting of the finest kind of food, was usually packed and brought out in big new washtubs. We would sit down and eat, and believe me it always tasted good. Then we spent a whole hour resting. How wonderful it was to lay down on the flat of your back and rest. Then it was back to work again and we worked until six in the evening. When you walked into the lobby and cleaned up and ate your supper (as we called it then) it did not take much persuasion to get the men to go to bed early. You did this day after day, and men worked at this kind of job and liked it. If you got $1.75 a day you were getting good wages. I can remember when I got $1.25 a day. I can also remember when I got 50¢ a day. I can remember when I hoed corn for 25¢ a day. I can also remember when I was glad to work for my meals and a place to sleep, yes those were what some call the "good old days."

> I muse about those "yesterdays"
> Through which the world has grown;
> And I prize their contributions
> And the seed that they have sown.
> But though my years be four-score-ten,
> And life a joyful lay,
> My opportunities begin
> And end with my "Today."

A Happy Time Singing Together

Some of those were days that might be considered prophetic of things today. We had broadcasting, plenty of it in those days, in which people all over the country listened to our music. There was a telephone company that put in lines and phones; and there was what would be called a party line on which there were as many as 25 or 30 or more telephones on the same line covering many, many miles. They were all battery-operated, since there was no electricity in those days in that part of the country. In fact, it has only been in very recent years that the powerlines reached the rural areas in which I grew up. It was understood that there were certain calls that were emergency calls on the telephone and when something unusual happened, something we wanted everyone to know about or hear, there was one call of six long rings which meant everybody should listen in.

Often we gathered together at one of the homes with our musical instruments. I played in those days a banjo, guitar, mandolin, and I tried the accordian, the organ, and even the violin; however, I never went too far with the violin. Of the string instruments I think the banjo was my favorite. In my adult years I learned to play the handsaw which has a tone similar to the violin.

We would meet in these homes and give six rings on the telephone to call up the community. People would lay their telephone receivers on top of the telephones and would listen and phone their requests in. We would play for hours, though never later than midnight or 1:00 a.m., and it consisted entirely of singing and music on the instruments. I do not recall any requests we could not play or sing, a little anyway. These were real music parties and everyone enjoyed them very much. They were usually held in one of the larger homes, but no one ever suggested turning them into a dance. I wish we could go back to some of them now as in those days.

Our music parties included Sunday afternoons, but no musical instruments were played on Sunday. Nor did we have ball games on Sunday, but we would gather at the church or under a maple tree at a certain home depending on the weather and sing for hours. We didn't know much about music, but everybody there could carry a tune and could make their own parts. I guess it would be called "country music" today. No instruments were permitted in the church, so when our songfests were in the church we just sang.

Now and then someone would come in that knew or understood music, and we would have a singing school, learning to sing by shape note, uncultivated voices by people who knew nothing about the rudiments of music . . . but what a happy time singing together.

"Preacher"

Having begun very early in life to read the scriptures, I spent a great deal of time reading my Bible and committing to memory many, many portions of scripture, which has been a great help to me in my ministry. It was easy in my daily conversations with my friends to get me started talking on the subject of religion during which I would quote the scriptures to them, sometimes to their delight, sometimes to their surprise and sometimes to their chagrin. Very early I was nicknamed the "preacher." I did not join in many of the games and things that many of the others joined in doing. I was made fun of and laughed at a great deal because of my nickname "preacher." This seemed to set me apart and I was not readily accepted in the inner circle except where they needed me or wanted me to play an instrument, sing or make up a ball team. I could run, play various musical instruments, sing and make a speech if need called for it. So I was accepted in those fields rather eagerly because of my ability to do those things. This left a void in my early life that never seemed to be filled, due perhaps to not having any real close boyhood friends to share those values that were dear to me. However, I have never regretted the decisions that set me apart. Early in life I learned to know what the scriptures meant by "And Jesus said a prophet is not without honor save in his own country."

I had another ability that stood me in good stead many times in my earlier days. In spite of the fact that there were 65 or more pupils in the school which I attended, the little red school house, I was the champion racer. This kept me from getting into a lot of trouble which I would have suffered from had I not been able to outdistance some of my friends who were determined to force me to do things that I did not want to do. So I would escape. For instance, one day as I walked alone along the road on my way home I heard the voices of some of the community boys ahead of me, laughing, shouting, screaming, and crying out in delirious fashion, and I knew that they were drinking. I had never gotten into the habit and I was determined not to ever begin. There were three of them and when we met they began to laugh about the "preacher," offering me the bottle. I refused and one of them said, "Well, this is one time you're going to take a drink." So the three of them converged upon me to force me to take a drink from their bottle. I do not know what was in it but it was surely something that made them act peculiar and I did not want any part of it. I guess I was quick enough as I escaped on swift feet like a deer and got away from them. I was thankful that I was in good practice. I could relate other events such as this, however, there were many good times and happy memories that stay with me.

The Daily Roundup

A chore that marked a pleasurable event in my early days was that of herding the neighborhood cattle. Everybody owned a cow or two which they did not fence in but, after milking them in the morning, turned them out and they would gather together in a herd and wander over the mountainside in search of feed. It was what was called "open range." It was agreed by the neighborhood people that we would take turns in hunting the cattle, in rounding up the herd and bring them in for milking and the night. My turn would come about every two or three weeks and I would herd the cattle for one entire week, then someone else would take their turn. So it went day after day, week after week. Starting from home at about 2:30 or 3:00, my dog and I would go off to the mountains—sometimes with my gun, sometimes without it—and we would wander over the mountainside in search of the herds. They were very, very ingenious. Sometimes they were easy to find; other times not so easy.

All of the cattle wore bells, but all of them knew how to keep their bells silent, especially on a rainy day. They would find a secluded spot, lie down and hold their bells still and chew their cuds.

It was only by accident that they would move their heads and you would hear the bells. I would have to search sometimes for hours before I could hear the tinkle of a bell, sometimes as far as five miles from home. This would happen often on the rainy days when it was most disagreeable to hunt in the woods for cattle. Then when they got started for home there was no difficulty at all in getting them to their respective owners. In fact, they were good travelers and when I got lost in the woods they would lead me home.

Sometimes I would have to seize one of the cattle by the tail and run to keep up, but they always brought me home. I was glad for the pathfinders that the cows turned out to be.

We had one or two cows of our own, cultivated and domesticated to such an extent that I would get them by the bell collar and lead them wherever I wanted them to go, and this I would often do.

Finally the herd would arrive at the various forks of the mountain road from which each cow on her own would amble off to her home to be fed, milked and closed in a pen or barn until the following morning. Then the process began all over again, day after day especially during the months of the year in which there was some grass or vegetation for them to feed on.

My Dog, Sport

It was a pleasure in those days to wander over the mountainside in this fashion, for I learned to know the book of nature better than I would have any other way. There were some things about it that made me vigilant the rest of my life. It was a country filled with rattlesnakes, as I mentioned earlier. Sometimes one would be in my pathway, curled and ready to strike before I realized it. Fortunately, I never got bit and I learned how to handle them. I eliminated many a one by just the simple means of employing what technique I knew, with the help of my little dog.

Now I would like to say something in behalf of that little dog. His name was Sport. He was not a pedigreed dog. I do not know what breed he was. He was just an ordinary kind of dog, but in intelligence he was pedigreed. He learned obedience and would obey better than most people.

There were times when I wanted him to stay home when I went places, and believe it or not, all I needed to do was tie him up with a twine string and say to him, "Now Sport, you stay home," and when I got back he was still tied up and waiting for me.

The same thing was true of my father who dug

coal sometimes. He was just as obedient for my father when my father took him along. Father would dig coal for the neighbors for their winter heat. He would dig it for 1¢ a bushel and run it out on what he called the dump for an extra 3¢ a bushel. Many times I have known him to dig as much as 100 bushel for that price. He was usually kept busy digging coal to the extent of time he had to give to that work.

Now our little dog Sport always wanted to go to the mines to be with him. He would go inside and lie down on a cushion as close to Dad as he could get and he would stay there until he went home. No twine string would hold him at home now; it took a good strong chain to keep him home when Dad was going to the mines to dig coal. Somehow or other Sport sensed there was danger and he might be needed to go for help in case of an accident.

We Become Lumberjacks

I mentioned earlier that I grew up in what might be considered a virgin forest; a forest in which no living person at that time could remember timber ever being cut. Chestnut trees were growing thick all over the country and they had grown to such tremendous sizes that you would not believe if I were to attempt to give dimensions. I shall describe one or two anyway because it is the truth.

I remember finding what I thought was a bee hive in a large chestnut tree. I told my Dad and my Uncle Jim Byrd about it and we went to inspect the tree. It was almost beyond the nerve of anyone to attempt to cut the tree because of its size, but finally it was decided that we would cut it in order to get the honey.

We had a seven foot crosscut saw, so we got the saw and a double bit axe and began sawing. We had to saw a ways and then cut a notch in the tree so the saw would not bind and would move back and forth. This had to be repeated time after time. The tree, after an hour or more, finally fell to the ground. It was a dead tree and we went down to the top of the tree to find the bees and hopefully the honey. But alas we found that I had discovered a tree with a big nest of yellow jackets in it!

There were other trees that were still larger than this. I can remember later when the lumber company came in to cut out the timber there was one that they cut down which was defective at the base. They had to cut off a matter of ten or twelve feet of it before they could get anything solid enough to warrant keeping. The part they cut off was hollow at the base. I am 5'6" tall and I could walk into the hollow of that tree. That size tree was common over the country.

It is indeed now just a memory and challenges one's imagination to even think of trees of that size growing in that country, but they did and I grew up among them. In clearing our little patch of land there were some large chestnut trees that needed to be cut. Most were dead; some even lying on the ground. They had to be disposed of. Most were solid enough to make rails. One large tree was lying just above the house we had built, so we decided to make rails from it. We took the same saw I mentioned we used in cutting down the supposed bee tree and started cutting. It took us over an hour to successfully cut off one log. Dad would get up on the tree where it lay on the ground and cut awhile, then he would get down and I would take his place on the tree and cut. We repeated this process until we had the log cut off.

When we cut it up we made wooden wedges with which to split the log and divided it up into

10 or 12 foot rails. It really made a pile of them. The residue of the tree being too rotten to make anything else, was piled up and then the first rainy day that came it was burned. Dad discovered that it was easier to burn a log heap on a rainy day than on a dry day. I do not know what the charm was. It seemed to work that way and so we cleared up the land in this manner.

The forest supplied logs and lumber from which to build our homes, fence the fields, fuel to keep us warm and cook our food, which we raised on the cleared land.

Serving Death Notices to Bees

Another novel custom current in those days many of you have heard of I'm sure. When clearing up the land we would have first a slashing. A slashing was when the trees were felled, trimmed up, and cut into logs. Then later a log rolling would be announced. The people from all over the community were considered invited to the log rolling. A good thrasher's dinner was always a part of these events. As many as 15 or 20 men would come to help not only with the slashings and log rollings, but with the building of a house or barn whichever the case might be. This of course was repeated as each man had need. The entire community responded; seldom did anyone work alone at clearing a piece of land, or building homes and barns. It was a mutual concern to everybody in the community to take an interest, and the work was done in true neighborly style.

This was repeated likewise whenever a man raised a bumper crop of corn. We would have what was called a corn shucking in which the people of the community were invited to gather and shuck corn. They did not meet until about 8:00 in the evening or as soon as it was damp enough for the corn to "shuck out." The ears of corn would fly until the shocks were all dragged in and the corn was all shucked. On these occasions, usually not a bumper dinner was served, but apple pie, cake and cider for refreshments, and everybody had a good time.

Many other peculiar customs could be mentioned in connection with those days, among which were the customs accompanying funerals. When someone died in the community they didn't send for a funeral director for there were no funeral directors; the people took care of those things themselves. There were usually local people who came into the home, measured the body, went back and manufactured a coffin—coffin mind you, not a casket—brought the coffin to the home, placed the body in it, and in the absence of embalming fluid, used salt water and alum to preserve the body. Customarily, the night before the funeral there was held what was known as the "wake." The people in the community gathered together and stayed up all night with the family to keep them company. A lot of coffee, pie, cake and usually some cider was served during the "wake."

At the funeral it was the custom to watch very carefully so as to know who was going to be buried next. If in the course of the filling of the grave someone picked up a shovel first, the next death would be a woman; if they picked up a mattock first, it would be a man who would be buried next.

Another belief—if the family in which the

death occurred had honeybees, immediately after the death of the individual, the bees had to be fully informed, otherwise the bees would all leave or die. They firmly believed in this. I once wrote down while I was in school the many different superstitions that governed the lives of the people of those days. I could remember 50 superstitions that were in vogue then.

Forward We Must Go

We stand upon the threshold of an age that's past and gone
And turn our faces forward to a new one that must come.
We hold within our memories, the scenes and days of yore
But joyfully we turn our hearts to face an open door.
Our fathers builded memories in those golden days now past.
But we are building memories of a future not yet cast.
We gladly hold the memories that remain within the maze,
But we're building for our children memories of the better days.
Choose then with care, O builder,
Words and deeds of noble strain,
That the future may record that you
Have builded not in vain.

PART THREE

My Little Sister

In attempting a venture like this it seems that one's life falls into natural divisions. This brief story of my life is no exception.

One of the most important events of my life happened to me at age 16. Until then I was an only child, but when I was 16 my parents decided to take into their home a little girl named Myrtle whose mother had recently died. They were hopeful that they might even be able to adopt her.

After some time, however, the child's father decided to remarry and he came to reclaim his daughter. To give her up was a great blow to my mother and she was very heartbroken and grieved.

As strange as it may seem, but also as it often happens in life, within a year afterwards there came into our home a real flesh and blood sister. She was also named Myrtle—Myrtle May. There was a little over 16 years difference in our ages. At first I was very unhappy because she had robbed me of my throne and the center of my parents' life.

I soon grew to tolerate her, however, then to like her, and before long to love her very, very much, and I still do. She has always been my little sister and I her big brother. She is now a nurse and lives in Pittsburgh.

A Big Step

The years slipped by without my goal of more education and training in preparation to become a minister being realized. There were no rural high schools in the section of the country where I lived, and distance and cost prevented me from attending those that may have been in the city. None of my friends or acquaintances had gone to school above the eighth grade, nor was I encouraged to pursue any further education.

In fact, my parents were very much against my going away to school, as were the church leaders of my district. Yet, in face of all opposition I had made up my mind it was something I must do. There had been some visiting ministers and church workers that encouraged me and even informed me of a church-related school at Nokesville, Virginia.

Until this time I had not been away from home for more than two weeks at a time, and then only a distance of 75 miles. So it was a very great step for me to take.

When I had gathered all the money I could manage and packed a small suitcase with a very limited wardrobe, I went to the local train stop at Newlington, West Virginia, and bought a one way ticket to Nokesville.

So in the fall of 1919 I found myself arriving with the sum of $2.00 left in my pocket, and being met by a Mr. Franklin Byer, the principal of Hebron Seminary, located at Nokesville, Va. This was the beginning of a new venture for me, my first year of high school in a strange situation, among strange people. I was something like Robinson Crusoe, although there were a lot of new people to meet and friends to make. I must admit I was very homesick and the school term seemed a long one.

Among the friends I made while at Hebron Seminary were Guy West, Russell West, Isaac Sanger, Saylor Cubbage, I. N. H. Beahm and many others. If I could name them all, you who read this would remember and know some of whom live among us even now.

Here I was without even money to buy books, but I had been promised that I could find work, as there were plenty of jobs available in that area. I worked at any job that I could get and needed doing. I operated a carbide plant that funished all the lights for the school; I carried groceries; I acted as janitor; and in between times, I worked out on the farms wherever I could find a job.

And of course I went to school and studied, thankful and happy that at last I was among a group of people who were interested in the same things I was. I was also grateful that I could continue the study of the Bible, as well as other subjects that were included during the school term.

When spring came and the close of school, I had saved up enough money to buy a ticket back home and to a happy reunion with my family and friends.

Wedding Bells

During the summer I had some contact with and information about the Academy that was connected with Bridgewater College, at Bridgewater, Va. This was somewhat nearer to my home than Nokesville, so I decided to attend Bridgewater for my second year of academic work. I well remember arriving in the fall of 1920 on the Chesapeake and Western train from Harrisonburg, Va., a railroad which was affectionately referred to as the "crooked and weedy."

Upon my arrival, I had no one to guide me as to what I should do or what courses to take. In fact, my entrance into academic work was met with a straightforward question, "What do you want to take?," and even though I was 22 years of age, I had no way of knowing what that should be. I do know that I cannot recall a time when I did not want to be a minister.

The ministry was uppermost in my mind from my early childhood and I said so, but I was not advised what courses to take to achieve my desire. I was eventually told that there were certain groups of studies that I had to take in order to graduate. From these I selected what was required, and after that and some prayer and meditating I selected others that were Bible related.

I do not know how I got along as well as I did. Of course it was necessary for me to work to pay my way during the school term, which I earned at anything I could find to do—around the school grounds, in the kitchen and out on the farms.

The end of another school year finally came and I made my way back to my home in Usphur County, W. Va., stopping in Buckhannon, W. Va., to visit friends. Also visiting in that home was a missionary deputation team, including a young lady by the name of Doris Ann Hartley whom I admired very much. We started a correspondence and I called on her as often as I could which wasn't as often as we wished, since she lived in the northern section of the state and some distance away.

Nevertheless, our courtship progressed to the point that we were married in the fall, September 5, 1921, at the very same place where we first met.

Dynamite

> I was young but I remember,
> In the days of twenty-one,
> It was in the mild September;
> Autumn work had just begun.
> In a little country hamlet
> Where I'd spent most of my life,
> Where I got to sort o' thinking
> What I needed was a wife.

I was twenty-three that winter,
But my hair was getting thin;
I was just a youthful splinter
With some fuzz upon my chin.
Up to then I'd been contented,
Never seemed on mischief bent;
Lived at home like Uncle Silas
And to town I never went.

Patiently I lived and waited,
Roaming o'er the country side;
All the girls in town I dated,
None of them could be my bride.
For the girl that I would marry,
One that I would one day love,
Would have dimples like a cherry
And be gentle as a dove.

Grey eyes, too, I think I wanted,
Tall and slender neat and fair,
Courage like a knight, undaunted,
Having red and wavy hair;
Wouldn't smoke or chew tobacco,
Bake the most delicious cakes,
Be a he-man if she had to,
Wouldn't be afraid of snakes.

Well, I met her at convention,
Ne'er so glad in all my life
When I told her my intention
And she said she'd be my wife.
So, we married come a Monday,
I had found my choice at last;
Life was one big happy Sunday
Once with her my lot I'd cast.

And I'd found the one I wanted,
Tall and straight and wondrous fair,
Like Napoleon undaunted
And she had red wavy hair.
And the dimples, well, she had 'em,
Twinkled out like stars at night;
But the whole of her anatom'
Was chuck-full of dynamite.

But say, if I should ever make it,
Ever gain success in life,
Wish for fame or wealth, and take it,
I will owe it to my wife.
She instilled the inspiration
Which equipped me for the fight,
For what I needed in my station
Was a charge of dynamite.

Fifty-three years we've been married,
Still I'm happy and content;
Never once has she but tarried,
To hard tasks has willing went.
Still she cooks and washes dishes,
Labors far into the night;
Reigns supreme o'er all my wishes;
Still she's full of dynamite.

A New Life

At this point my career changed once again, because I was not now at liberty to do as I pleased; now I had to secure a job to support a wife, which I managed to do. I got a job cutting timber at $1.75 per day not including board. Later I worked in the coal mines for some eight years. It was during that time that our son and only child was born, Ernest Lee Byrd, December 21, 1923.

Mining in those days was not easy. You worked under very difficult conditions with poor pay and for the most part less than desirable living conditions. The mine in which I worked at the time of our son's birth was no exception. While we lived in a company-owned house, which was rather new, it was just a shell upon stilts high enough to park a car under. There was a coal stove for heat and for cooking.

How clear in my mind is the night Ernest Lee was born, at home with the company doctor in attendance. The physician had to ride a horse to get to the house due to the mud being too deep in the dirt road to cross on foot. Then it turned cold and was so cold that a glass of water would freeze solid beside the bed in which mother and son lay.

Ernest survived, although the doctor thought he might not.

In 1929 we found ourselves living near Wheeling, W. Va., working on a farm as well as in the mines there. We raised vegetables and sold the surplus in Wheeling and in the nearby mining town; also we took care of the farm and feeder-cattle for the owner.

The desire of becoming a pastor was always uppermost in my mind and to do this I knew I must continue my education. So the decision was made to return to school in order to complete high school and college. I am not certain about the manner of persuasion, but it seemed an inner compulsion that forced me to make that sort of decision, and I made it with my wife consenting.

It was decided that we could enroll in the academy at Daleville, Va., but how would we get there? We had no means of transporting our household goods which we would need once we arrived. We did have a Ford touring car but the move required a truck of some kind.

"The Model T"

I was baptized at the age of thirteen, and had now been a minister in the Church of the Brethren for some years, preaching and teaching Sunday School wherever we happened to be living. There was ample opportunity and need for my services. We had made friends at the local Methodist Church and I was teaching a class there. I shall never forget one of God's men, a little man, very small of stature, but very friendly, helpful, and neighborly in his attitude toward me. His name was Harvey Trumbull and he lived on a rather large farm not too far from the church.

When he learned of my decision and need for transportation, he came to me one day and said, "Well, I have a truck that I will trade you very, very reasonably. It's a Model T truck, four cylinders, magneta type, no lights on it, no battery, but it runs well; is in good shape. It has a cattle rack on it and you can load a lot of stuff on it." (It turned out to not have been in too good shape for a long trip out on the road).

When I inquired as to what he wanted for it, he surprised me out of my wits by telling me he would trade the truck for 25 of my chickens that we had on hand. So I agreed at once and the trade was made. I began immediately repairing the rack that was on the truck and got it in shape so we could load all of our household belongings on it. The trip then of about 400 miles would begin as soon as proper arrangements could be made.

A cousin, Clifford Land, who was staying with us for awhile agreed to accompany me on the trip over the mountains from Wheeling, W. Va., to Daleville, Va., to attend the Daleville Academy located 11 miles north of Roanoke, Va. Norman Seese was the principal of the school and had paved the way for our coming.

Preparation was started for the big event. First, I had to move my parents back to their home in Upshur County. They had moved temporarily near to us and my father was working at the carpenter trade. This move made, we began in earnest to sort and pack for our trip over the mountains. My wife's brother, Dewey, consented to drive our Model T Ford, which was loaded with as many breakable things as possible, along with my wife, our son, Ernest, and our dog, Watch, a very good gentle watch dog and company for our son. I loaded the truck with all our belongings, including 65 young laying hens in crates, which would help us with our living expense once we arrived at our new home. We started with the truck a day or so in advance of the car, thinking we'd get together on the road at some point.

A Seven Day Nightmare

Most of the roads were not paved, but gravel, and we had to take a longer route to make the trip. I do not know, now that I think back over the experience, what possessed me to think that I could ever make the trip over the Applachian Highlands, the Alleghenies, with a truck of that type. However, my desire for more education and training was greater than any fear I may have had.

I was mechanically inclined and I could reline brakes and make other minor repairs, which unfortunately I needed to do time after time. The first day we made it to Waynesboro, Pa., where we spread our bed upon the ground and spent the night. Strangely enough, we were not molested by policemen or anyone else. Early the next morning we started on our way again. Grafton, W. Va., was our next stop and there we ran into some severe difficulties. A rear main bolt in the motor had stripped a thread, so it became necessary for us to pull the motor entirely out of the truck to replace the bolt. To do this we had to pull off of the main road for a place to park. Here is where my wife passed us in the car, and we never got together on the road nor for several days after they reached Daleville.

It is very fresh in my mind, how I worked up until two in the morning on that motor and then did not get it finished. I was having great difficulty trying to get the triple gears back together. A little boy was standing by and after awhile he said, "You know how my Dad does it?" I said "No" and he continued, "He takes a string," and he showed me how to take a twine string and tie it around the triple gears. I did as he said; they dropped on and soon I had the job finished. I put the motor back together, strained the oil to get the burned out brake linings out of it, and we started on our way again.

The next stop was near Junior, W. Va. (where we lived later in pastoral work for nine years). Here we slept under an overhanging rock. The next stop or night was near Durbin, W. Va. (where again we later lived, serving churches there). A main bearing burned out which I replaced with a new one. However, this one did not last very long until it also burned out, which meant another stop, another repair job and night under the stars. I had to put an old bearing back in and again strain the oil. Then we pursued our way. I had begun to feel like Job, but I kept on, repairing the truck, feeding the chickens and doing the best we could for ourselves.

Our next stop was just south of Staunton, Va., on Route 11. We stopped near a farmhouse to get permission to make our bed in an old building that was below the road. They would not permit us to do so, but they said, "We have good beds here in the house. You can come up and sleep in these beds." They insisted, so we accepted including a good supper, the first home cooked meal we had in six days.

On the seventh day of our travel we finally arrived at about 2:30 in the afternoon at Daleville, Va. When we arrived and I got out of the truck, I looked over the load and the tires. The tires took 90 pounds pressure. When I looked at the tire on the right rear wheel there was a great big knot on it, half as big as your head, just ready to blow out.

Fortunately we were at our journey's end and we pulled up in front of the house that we were to occupy during the school year and began to unload. Needless to say, my wife and son and her brother were very greatly relieved, as they had intended to start back on the way the next day in search of us. Since then I've wondered why we did not telephone to inform them where we were and what was delaying us. But for some reason we didn't. Let me say here we only lost one chicken, and that one got away at one of our stops and went to a nearby farmhouse. Later when we were pastoring a church in that same community, a young man who was just a boy when we traveled that route, recalled the incident of the runaway chicken and it was to his home it had gone. Every day I realize more and more what a small world we live in.

I stand upon the threshold of a day—
Ten thousand paths lead from my feet away
Each with an end, and at the end a prize
Which I must win or lose, my strength defies.
If I should win, 'Tis but because I will;
If I should fail, my place in life to fill.
If I should win or lose succeed or fail
Depends on me and how I set my sail.
God gave me strength, a bark, and yet a goal
And wisely made me captain of my soul.

PART FOUR

A Second Chance

The fall of 1929 I was once again back on the road in securing a formal education. Norman Seese was principal of Daleville Academy. He was very helpful to us in coming to the school and during our stay there. The work was no less difficult, however, there was still plenty of it.

The cousin who accompanied me on this adventurous journey, stayed on with us for a while. He attended school and worked until he decided to return home because of financial difficulties. My wife's brother also returned home after visiting and seeing some of the country around Daleville.

Now we were on our own. Having been properly enrolled in the Academy, classes began for us both. Since our son, Ernest, was not old enough to enter public school, he took turns going to class with us, which he enjoyed very much. The teachers would often ask him some questions and surprisingly enough he would come up with some very good answers.

I was able to find work about the school and in the "Nininger Orchards." Permission was given to me for cutting wood from the woodlands nearby. This was used to heat the house and to cook with. In a small building in the back we housed our chickens—hens, which we had relied on to help us with expenses, and we were not disappointed.

My wife helped in various ways, doing laundry for the students and making candy to sell. She relied on Rev. Frank White for transportation to Roanoke, as he made weekly trips to that city to sell his produce. He was very helpful to us in marketing our eggs and an occasional hen that was culled from the flock, the money from which we used to supplement our income. Brother White, as he was fondly called, fired the boilers and did various other things about the school, and his wife cooked for the students. They were both very friendly and helpful to us and also to others. He wore a beard and both he and Sister White had the philosophy of life that characterized the Church of the Brethren some years back. We shall always remember and cherish Brother and Sister White.

Another Move

At the end of the school year, 1930, it was rumored that Daleville Academy would not open the following year. (Actually it did continue for one or two years longer.) We were, therefore, up against the proposition of finding a place to go, and if I wanted to continue my schooling we had to find another school. One day J. H. Ruebush from Shenandoah College at Dayton, Va., visited the school and, learning of our need, offered us such an attractive proposition that we immediately decided to come to Shenandoah College to finish high school.

A house was provided for us and as soon as it could be arranged we hired the man to whom I had sold the old Model T truck that brought us over the mountains the previous year to move us to Dayton, our new home. We were houseparents to eleven young men. They were jolly good young folk, at times a bit noisy, but we got along and enjoyed them very much.

The college had several cows which they had taken in trade for expenses of some students who could not have attended school otherwise. These cows had been brought in from the mountains and never been stabled before. I was given charge of them, and I had quite a time getting them broken to the stable and teaching them to stand still long enough to be milked. I also mowed the grass and did several other jobs around the school. I discovered that I would have a very heavy schedule in order to graduate, since some of my subjects from previous schools would not transfer.

My wife in addition to attending school also helped with the cooking for a student body of some 250. The football team were served double portions! I should not neglect to mention the coal and wood range was still being used. The cooks often had to go out and split and chop their own wood.

Our son, Ernest, of course, was making life lively with his jolly antics. He began his first year of elementary school at Dayton. Also here the much loved watch-dog was run over by a truck and killed to all our sorrow and especially to Ernest. He was a great companion for him and Ernest missed him very much.

This school year was a great experience for us all. We treasured the friendships and the opportunity to continue in school.

A Higher Goal

At the end of the school year, 1931, another milestone had been reached. I had finally graduated from high school, however, my goals were set higher. I had made application to attend Bridgewater College. Late in the summer I had not received a satisfactory answer, and had almost given up hope. Just a few weeks before the opening of the fall term at Bridgewater the president, Dr. Paul H. Bowman, and Mrs. Bowman drove up in front of where we were living, rushed in quickly, handed me a contract and permission to enter as a student. The contract included taking care of Cole Hall, the library and some day students rooms, for which I was to receive $125 a year toward my tuition.

My wife also received a contract to take care of Yount Hall and Rebecca Hall at the rate of $22.50 a month for ten months of the year. We had to depend mostly on her income for groceries and other needs, so it was necessary to supplement this in other ways. We bought a washing machine from the Hawkin's Hardware Company at Harrisonburg, making monthly payments. Some months there was no money for payments, then they just charged us the interest. Doris did laundry for the students, some weeks as many as 50 and 60 white shirts, plus the other things that went along with the weekly wash. Two students got laundry done free for picking up and delivering. Others paid 50¢ a washload; however, several would double up on her and get theirs for free. She had a unique way to re-seat pants from the fronts of vests and had many calls for this from the students.

We were furnished a house, the old infirmary building, which had power and water, but no heat. So again I cut the trees that needed to be taken out for wood. We were still using the old wood heating and cooking stoves. When wood was scarce, we used anything we could find to burn: walnuts, dried balls of newspapers, etc. Here in this building we spent the next four years. The house was known from then on as the "Bird House." The gymnasium stands on the same spot now. The four years of college were difficult years; however, I was glad to have the opportunity of going forward with the education I desired and knew I had to have to become an effective pastor. I was grateful for this open door.

The Lures of Life

I've long since heard of the lures of life,
The lure of the open door;
The lure of love and the lure of strife
And the lure of a distant shore.
I've heard of the lure of the open sky.
The lure of the unsupposed.

But the lure for which I'd rather die
Is the lure of the door that's closed.

I've heard of the lure of the mountain steep,
The lure of the unexplored;
The dangerous lure of the ocean's deep;
The heights that are not yet soared.
I've heard of the lure of the golden clime,
And the lure of the land unrosed;
But the lure of that seems the most divine
Is the lure of the door that's closed.

Men scale the heights of the mountain peak,
They dive to the ocean's deep;
In the pits of earth men love to seek,
From the tallest steeples leap.
Men press their way to the great unknown
Unfettered by sky or shore.
And I've waxed convinced, as I've older grown,
He can open that long-closed door.

College and More

The next four years I was on a very rigid schedule. At one time my wife was very ill and in bed for several months. I had to do most of the housework, help get our son ready for school, do my work around the buildings and attend classes. My mother came to help out for a short time. Afterward my wife's sister, Virginia, came and took over the work which my wife had been doing. She brought with her a little daughter, Deloris, whom my wife could care for while she was out at work. This small child we grew to love. She spent much time with us over the years and now seems like a daughter to us. After some time my wife was once again able to resume her work and we continued on through the four years of college.

In addition to the work already mentioned I was assigned the duty of night watchman. This was not advertised but it was thought by the officials that it would keep to a minimum some of the problems on campus that were undesirable and in violation of the rules of the school, and indeed it did seem to help.

I may sound like a broken record on that word, work, but it seemed to follow me wherever

I went. I did not resist or object as WORK was the instrument that made it possible for me to keep open the door to higher education. So I worked at whatever I could find to do.

One summer I worked about the college grounds and also planted five gardens on shares. This helped greatly with a goodly amount of vegetables to eat during the summer and to can for winter. I have often said that the Heifer Project started here. One summer, the Harry Edmonsons loaned us a milk cow which not only supplied us with all the milk, butter and cheese we could use, but an extra amount to share with some boys who were working on campus. The cow was staked on the athletic field where there was good grazing.

I continued to return to the Dayton Church to teach the same class I had taught while at Shenandoah College; also to take my turn at the various preaching points in the Cooks Creek Congregation.

During the next two summers I was employed by Mr. Lloyd Myers to open a service station at the edge of Harrisonburg. The business is still in operation and is owned by Lloyd's brother, Victor. After opening the service station, Lloyd decided to go into the trucking business and asked me to help him. He started with a six-ton truck, in which we traveled all over the country hauling freight to and from such cities as Philadelphia, Baltimore, Norfolk, Richmond and many other places. We were on the road together as much as

24 hours a day for which I was paid the sum of one dollar a day and board. It seemed a very low wage, but in the long run it paid off well.

We Live in a Tent

The summer after my junior year in college I was sent by the District Board in cooperation with the General Brotherhood Board of the Church of the Brethren to West Virginia as a summer worker. No salary was promised, but we were told that the churches in which we would work—Glady, Willdell, Bemis and Bowden—would supply us with food. We lived in a tent, at first sleeping on the ground. Later we were able to buy three army cots from Montgomery Ward. The tent was loaned to us by a good friend who lived near Dayton, Va., O. G. Whitmere. He also helped us out with food when we had none. How he would know just when help was most needed I do not know. Not only this summer but the next he and his wife came to our rescue when the larder was empty.

It was during this summer that our son, Ernest, broke his left leg in five places. We had to carry him many places, but there was no thought of giving up. One of the churches had no road into it, so we were met with a workcar on the railroad, piling on the things we would need while there, our little dog, and the three of us. How good it felt to sleep in a real bed and eat at a well-spread table, the only place we could do this during the summer, except for the occasional invitations for meals by some of the church folk. At the end of the summer, we were invited to spend the last week with the Boyd Phares family at the Bowden church. The temperature had dropped below freezing in the mountains and the tent became rather uncomfortable.

During this summer we held Bible schools, revival services, music classes and got a lot of experience which would be a great help to us later. At the end of the summer we were paid the amount of $75. How much that amount would have helped at the beginning or during the summer, no one could ever know!

Having no money we wondered how to buy supplies for Bible School. Then we decided we could ask each family to give ten cents, and with this we bought the supplies we needed. Some families, however, thought it was a waste of money and paper to do the handiwork which we used in our teaching of the children.

Sometimes some one would need transportation into Elkins, W. Va., the closest town of any size, and would buy some gas for the car, enough so that we were able to get around from place to place. Yet, we were among wonderful people. This was 1934, mid-Depression years, and there just was no money, nor was there anyone or board or committee to speak for us. Our inexperience kept us from speaking for ourselves, so we kept on, as we had dedicated ourselves to this type work. The Lord must have been watching over us very closely or we would never have survived those austere times. We give Him the praise.

Perhaps I should relate a few lighter moments during the summer. We were camped in the pasture field on a small island on which the Bowden church was located. One day when we returned from Bible School we found that the mule which shared the field with us had gotten into our tent and had completely consumed every eatable thing we had, and some things that were not so eatable, like the soap. It seems amusing now, but then it was a catastrophe.

Another time we were awakened late at night and told that the Cheat River, by which we were camped, was rising and we should go to a nearby home for the rest of the night.

Just prior to a baptismal service at which a number of folk were to be baptized in the river, a certain man sent me word that if I went ahead and baptized his wife, he would be there and shoot me. One has mixed feelings at a time like this. However, I went ahead with the service, she was baptized, and I wasn't shot.

At one point, some weeks after our son had broken his leg, the doctors decided a new cast would have to be put on. So this was done. However, with the green, wet, plaster cast and the cool temperature through living outdoors he became ill and suffered to the extent that it was decided that my wife should bring him back to Bridgewater for a period of time. The local physician, John D. Miller, had to split the entire cast open and cut several holes in it to relieve the pressure spots on his leg and foot.

Later, when they returned and we had gone up to the Widell church he was able to leave off the cast and walk on crutches. When we left this place and returned to our camp we left the cast behind to his delight! But lo! One morning some days later the good people at Widell came bringing it to us, thinking it was still needed. Our son hobbled to the nearby river and threw it in. Much to our surprise, a few mornings later we saw floating on the water what looked like a monster, or something from outer space. The cast, water-soaked, had swollen to twice its size and surfaced, with the holes looking like huge eyes!

The Great Achievement

At the close of the summer it was back to Bridgewater and school. This was my senior year. I was voted class poet and also asked to write a short verse for each of the seniors. I continued my schedule of classes, work, teaching Sunday School and preaching when called on.

What a wonderful day when June 3, 1935, arrived. I received my diploma, and realized the accomplishment of the past years and the fulfillment of the dreams of my earlier days of being better trained as a minister! I treasure that diploma and all the experiences and struggles that went along with gaining it and reaching this point in my life.

Longing

> To walk with Him the winding path
> That leads to heights above,
> To hear the still small voice
> That tells the meaning of His love;
> To know that though the cross is near
> The path our feet must tread,
> It's sombre spectre holds no fear
> Nor casts one ray of dread.
> To live within the limits

Of His love and never stray,
To let Him hold my faltering hand
And gently lead the way;
To hear the symphony of Love
Peal forth in harmony
With every heartbeat, every thought
And set the captives free—
This is my prayer.

PART FIVE

At the Sound of a Trumpet

Now for a place in which to serve the Lord. There was a denominational plan to place an executive secretary (then called a "Field Man") in the Second District of West Virginia, my home district. I had been asked to take the job. However, plans were not completed, and when they were, I was not to begin this work until the fall.

So in the interim we went to the little patch of ground on which my father had moved a rustic cabin, and started work on a church camp. It had been decided during our past summer's work there that this should be done for the young people. We had a small tract of land for which we had traded a rather large hog, raised by hand from a very small pig. We offered this piece of land located in Upshur County near Queens, W. Va., to the district for a church camp.

We left Bridgewater with as much baggage as the car would hold and took up our summer's work. Our son was with us, of course, and once again experienced all the difficulties of pioneer living. First the land had to be cleared or enough of it for some tents and cabins. Many times I worked alone, other times the neighbors or some of the folk from nearby churches would come in to help. The Valley River church built a small log cabin from logs taken from the camp site.

My father, George R. Byrd, then in his late 60s, "rove" over 400 boards with a froe and drawknife from a large chestnut tree. With these boards we built a dining hall. This we named McCann Hall in memory of S. M. McCann whose boyhood home was only a few miles from the camp site, "Indian Camp Rock." Here were held many meetings by the Brethren as well as other denominations in the vicinity. This rock still stands and should be made a memorial to his memory.

The latter part of July we opened Camp Hope. Leaders came for the most part from Bridgewater, Va., and nearby. "Dad" Kale was a great help in this first camp. Indeed it had been from him, Dan West and Alvin Brightbill whom we had met at Camp Bethel that the dream began for a camp for the young people of the Second District of West Virginia, and to which district we had committed ourselves to return.

The campers came bringing vegetables and other foods and a small fee for those who could pay. Keep in mind this was the summer of 1935 in the mid-years of the Depression, but the camp was on its way and was a success; and it remained so during the next nine years. Then in 1944 we were transferred to northwest Canada and it was decided to move the camp to a more convenient location. It continues to this day to be located near Belington, W. Va., still bearing the original name, Camp Hope. We were not promised any pay nor did we receive any for that summer.

I doubt if the influence on the lives of those that attended Camp Hope in the early days could be measured. We had classes for all ages, the folk from the community attending day classes as well as the evening vespers, many walking for miles to get there. These were folk that had watched the camp grow out of the forest and had also helped it become a reality with their labor. It was "the camp in our community" and they were proud to have had a hand in it. This was a great training experience for many just starting in this type work as well as for those more advanced.

When I reflect back over those first days of Camp Hope, and compare them with other church camps established in recent years with accommodations similar to those we offered at Camp Hope, it would now seem that our "primitive" accommodations are really the most desirable after all. At the time there was much criticism from church leaders that we were too rustic with cabins, tents and the like.

I should like to mention a novel way I had to

let the community know when I would come to work during the summer. I had borrowed a trumpet from a friend and when I would arrive on the scene, from the hilltop I'd just blow it and shortly several folk would come from various directions to lend a hand. This policy I used the entire nine years I had charge of the camp and it never failed to work.

The first camp ended, almost finishing us off as well. The summer had been a very great ordeal for us all, especially for our son who had never regained full strength after his broken leg, and my wife who had been cook, camp mother, teacher and many other things. She also, due to exposure, contracted pneumonia.

A doctor was called from the closest town, Buckhannon, W. Va. He came by car as far as he could, then by foot toward the direction of the camp. He became lost and we heard this loud cry out of the night. "Hello, hello, help, anybody down there, where are you?" I took the oil lantern and went to his rescue, after getting him untangled from the vines and brush I guided him on into camp. From his little black bag he gave my wife some medicine that worked magic. After he gave us all some kindly advice and shared a cup of tea with us, he was again on his way, this time guided back to the road and his car by me and the lighted lantern.

The Executive Mansion

In the fall of 1935 we made plans to move to Junior, W. Va. into the "Mansion," a four room house heated by an open fireplace. Here for the first time we had a cook stove operated by natural gas. What a luxury after cooking on an outside open fire during the summer at camp.

The Valley River congregation was located at Junior, and it had been designated as the best location for the district executive secretary to live. It was centrally located, on a main road, near a railroad. It was also not too far from Elkins, W. Va., where there was a hospital and various businesses to supply our needs.

There was another reason for locating us here. Since the Valley River churchhouse had been built in 1870, it was in need of being replaced and in a more convenient location. I was asked to give priority to this project, to be part-time pastor of this church and to give special attention to the Goshen and Bean Chapel churches, as well as to serve the entire district.

The next nine years my schedule was to spend half-time out in the district and half-time in the Valley River congregation. (This district has now been included with the First District of W. Va.

and is known as the West Marva District.)

We quickly settled in, beginning the work in earnest. The General Brotherhood Board had promised us a salary of $400 for the first year, which amounted to $33.33 per month.

Our son, Ernest, who was now ready for the sixth grade, entered the school there. We found the winter much more severe than we had been used to in Virginia for the past six years, and it took a little time adjusting to the climate.

A Sharing Friend

It was at this time that the work I had done for and with Lloyd C. Myers of Harrisonburg, Va., for the sum of one dollar per day, began to pay off. I was giving full-time to the district work and there was no way I could supplement my income, nor to purchase another car which I badly needed. On one of my trips back to Bridgewater to a conference, Lloyd came up to me and said, "You need a better car and I know where one can be bought reasonably." He added, "I can't preach and I can't sing, but I can make money and I feel like it is my duty to help you with a car so long as you are engaged in the kind of work you are in. In this way I can have a part in the Lord's work and help you at the same time."

So for the next nine years Lloyd assisted me in securing a car when the need would arise. They were all used cars, but good cars. He helped us in so many ways, as did many others or we could not have continued in this type work. He lives still at Mt. Crawford, Va., not far from my home in Bridgewater; however, we seldom see each other as he had to give up driving, can hardly walk, and lives alone in a trailer. I am not much better off as I am now unable to drive and am confined to the house and in a wheel chair, but we do talk on the phone and occasionally get together for a visit.

Our Son, Ernest

When our son, Ernest, was eleven years old he became deeply interested in electronics. In fact, his interest became evident much earlier. Around five or six years of age he put together what they called a crystal set which you listened to with earphones. He would often share the earphones with Watch, the dog. He was given some discarded radios which he would tear up and rebuild, putting them in working order.

We had a neighbor, George Arbogast, who was a radio repairman for the community, having learned by experience and on his own. He and Ernest became good friends and he helped him in many ways to learn the trade. Later Ernest worked without pay for a radio shop in Elkins in order to learn. He progressed to the point that he built his own transmitter and receiver and became a registered Ham Operator.

At the end of high school he went to Harrisonburg, Va., and secured a job with the original Miles Music Company as a radio technician. He worked here until he was drafted into the U. S. Navy during World War II. He continued in the same field of radio, radar and other types of communication during his period of service in the

Navy. When he returned from the Navy he continued in electronic work, returning to the same firm in Harrisonburg. Eventually he was among the first television technicians in the Shenandoah Valley.

Words cannot express the sadness and helpless feeling I had when the day came to drive Ernest along with another young man to the bus station where they were to take the bus to the Induction Center for parts unknown. Nor the heartache a few days later when a paper box arrived with his civilian clothes which he would not now need. The next time we would see him, he would be dressed in the traditional sailor uniform.

They Sent Us Back His Clothes

They sent us back his clothes,
An empty suitcase, and a paper box;
The box contained his things—
His suit, his ties, his underwear, his socks,
His shirts and handkerchiefs
And all his shoes, and things—
They sent them back, because
He wouldn't need them now.

When mother opened up the box, she cried,
And I stood by with aching heart, and sighed;
I wish I could have cried, for then I know
I could have stood it better, but the blow
Had dried my tears, and in their place an ache
Which tongue cannot explain, nor time can take.

But as I stood and watched, with aching heart
His mother touched each thing with gentle art,
While on her face a look of bitter pain
No one can never know, except the one
Who's had the pain of parting with a son.

But now they'd sent us back his things
To haunt us with the memories of a son we had
But have no more—unless the God of Love
So wills to intervene, and send him back.

This is our prayer, for after all he's got a wife you know,
Who waits for him with anxious heart—and so
To plan a home, to work, to build and dream,
Our dreams all over in life's passing stream.

Dear God, we wonder when will conflict cease
And once again we know the ways of peace;
When will the world be free from needless woes,
Nor those we love need send us back their clothes.
Haste, haste the day—brotherhood of man—
When wars shall cease and he comes home again.

Before entering the Navy, Ernest had met a lovely young lady, from Brandywine, W. Va., by the name of Doris Louise Dice. They fell in love and became engaged. At the end of his "boot training" at Great Lakes, Illinois, while he was home on leave for a few days they were married, June 14, 1943, in the new church at Junior. I was asked to perform the ceremony, a lovely but sad event, as he had to return to duty the following day to Northwestern University where he was taking a special course in electronics. From there he was sent to Norfolk, Va., to New York City, then shipped out to parts unknown. We suspicioned that he was headed toward England and most certainly would be engaged in the invasion of Normandy Beach from which so many did not return. I shall never forget the long periods of waiting. We received letters only occasionally, and those were censored. Even when we heard we did not know exactly where he was. Indeed it was a very trying experience, as only those who have had to go through it can know.

PART SIX

North of the Border?

In the spring of 1944 we were asked by the General Mission Board to transfer to the Dominion of Canada, and begin a ministry at Irricana, Alberta, 40 miles north of Calgary.

We had now been located at Junior, W. Va., for nine years. The camp was established, the new Valley River church had been built and the membership had doubled in numbers. The district as a whole was growing. The Goshen church had also been rebuilt. The original building was torn down, the boards turned inside-out and put back on the frame, which had withstood the severe winds better than the outside and roof. The Goshen church was built in 1898, the year of my birth and was my home church. It still is in use during the summer months and for funerals, as it is the only church for miles around.

The Valley River church was larger and more modern than most of the district churches. It was dedicated in 1940, built mostly by volunteer labor. There were some rather skilled carpenters in the congregation, as well as others who had skills that were needed and were very helpful in such an undertaking.

One item I must mention was the way in which the foundation and basement was built. The Men's Fellowship, with the help of a member who had a mold for building blocks, made one-by-one enough blocks to lay the foundation and basement of the church.

As I look back on that project, I marvel that we were able to construct such a nice, large, adequate building with so few helpers and with so little money—"but they had a mind and will to work." Many conferences and various meetings were held there since it was centrally located. It was there during a group meeting that the word of the attack on Pearl Harbor came.

It was while at Junior that Doris and I took some time out during the winter months to attend Bethany Seminary. If a degree was not earned, a wealth of experience and knowledge was gained under the many dedicated teachers under whom we studied. It gave us new strength and inspiration to continue on in the mission of the church to which we had dedicated ourselves.

After a lot of soul-searching, deliberation, prayer and meditation, we decided to accept the call to Canada and began making plans to that end.

A New Country

On May 11, 1944, we arrived at our new home, Irricana, Alberta, Canada, and was met by a group of the parishioners at the manse with a hot meal all ready for us. We quickly got acquainted and, after some adjusting to the change in climate and elevation, began work in the two congregations. One church was eight miles due west, and the other just across the road from the manse.

We had left home with heavy hearts. Our son was out on the high seas; my wife's father very ill. (He died two days after we arrived in Canada.) My father was not well and neither of my parents were eager for us to go so far away. The trip was around 3000 miles as the crow flies and was pleasant and uneventful. We stopped in Chicago at Bethany Seminary for a day or two to reminisce on our days in school there. Then we rambled onward at a leisurely pace, since we were traveling by a small car which wasn't made for speed but served us well.

There was not an individual we knew among the folk there, but we soon learned to know a likeable and friendly people. We thoroughly enjoyed our entire stay, and count it among our most pleasant experiences we ever had in serving churches.

The summer passed quickly. There were services to be held at both churches, Bible schools, camp, district meetings, plus learning to know the membership, neighbors and also our way over the countryside.

In the autumn of this same year, word came that my father was very ill and that I should return home if at all possible. I was at a loss to know what to do. The church came to my rescue and gave me a leave of absence after learning of the seriousness of his illness and the need for my return. They even went the second mile and paid my expenses.

I traveled back home by train and as soon as I arrived I made arrangements to take my father to the doctor, who gave him a good examination. He then let his hands drop to his side and crestfallen turned away. He told me privately that my father had cancer of the liver and perhaps no longer than three months to live.

He died on November 20, 1944. I stayed with him until the end, as my help was needed in caring for him. Soon after I came back home to West Virginia, my wife had received a message that our son, Ernest, was returning via the east coast on his way to the west coast and would be at his wife's home in Brandywine, W. Va., for no longer than two or three days. This message had to come by letter since my parents lived in an isolated part of Upshur County with no phones and I had no transportation. I again was helped out by the neighbors, who took me to the nearest town where I caught a bus to within ten miles of Brandywine. From there, a state policeman took me the rest of the way. It was late at night and I was just in time to spend a few hours with him, as he had to be on his way to Oceanside, California, to his next assignment the following day.

Gratitude

O God, who on the beach of Normandy
Stood by, and stayed the power of shot and shell,
Accept our gratitude, and may Thy Love
Lead us across the years, in all things well.
For well we know, we merit not thy favor,
And many a well-loved son there fell and died,
Yet not because Thou deemest not to love them.
We cannot understand, we yet abide,
And must fulfill a destiny of honor.
'Tis but our debt to Thee, we cannot hide
Ourselves behind some slim excuse and rust;
We live and serve the best
Because we must.

Welcomed Through the Portals

When it became necessary for me to leave Canada and return to my parents' home in the States, my wife was left alone. She was the one who would feel the burden of giving some kind of leadership to the churches to which we had so recently been called. The board there quickly requested her to fill the pulpit. She often said she was drafted into the ministry, although gladly, as she had been a lay speaker for a long time, and quite good at it, I might say. So it was that she and Brother Jack Crawford, a lay minister, kept the work going until my return three months later. Now they had two ministers for the price of one.

She received so many inquiries about how my father was, as well as how I was faring, that she decided to mimeograph a letter and mail it out to the two congregations. This went over so well that I continued it and enlarged it to carry the schedule, news and a short message. This I kept up the entire four years we were there, mailing out as many as 500 copies weekly not only to the homes there, but to family members and friends who had moved a distance away. This congregational newsletter has continued over the years, as it proved very valuable in reaching the membership with the happenings of the churches and community. It was enlarged to several pages and mailed once a month.

Let me pause here and go back to the time of our entrance into Canada. I well remember as we pulled up to the little customs station that Sweetgrass, Montana, was on the U. S. side and Coots on the Canadian side. We had no difficulty passing through the U. S. Customs, as they are only interested in people who are returning. When we pulled up to the customs on the Canadian side we were greeted like old friends. As it was wartime, we had to have permission from my home draft board to leave the U. S. and the custom officials had been sent a letter from the Canadian church introducing us and notifying them of our expected arrival. When we handed our papers to the official, I well remember even his uniform. He looked at us and smiled and greeted us, saying, "Well, where have you been? We've been expecting you for the last several weeks." I explained we had been delayed by sickness in our families and making final plans to move. They looked our papers over and did not even inspect the car which was loaded to capacity.

Many other cars were being unloaded, suitcases opened and things pretty well looked over, even gasoline tested from their cars. One of the officials learned that we had things in common. He had a son in the Canadian Navy; we had a son in the U. S. Navy. Even the little dog which belonged to our son was waved on. This incident, however, has stood out in my mind ever since as an illustration of something that is mentioned in the Bible. It is said in one of the Epistles that some "men's sins go before them into judgment and some men's sins follow after." It seems to me that if you and I have our papers cleared and all of our spiritual possessions checked here, that when we finally get to the borderline between earth and heaven, the Customs officials, as compared with this illustration here, will look over our papers and see that they are in order and we will be welcomed through the portals without interruption.

Mountain Miracles

I will of necessity be referring back to the earlier chapters of this book, as it is extremely difficult to remember in order all the things that should be included. Even when I have come to the end, there will be many important events left out.

Our first winter in this new land had passed and spring was in evidence on the broad prairies. The farmers were polishing up their machinery in preparation to plant another crop, which consisted of grains and mostly wheat. Land was measured in sections, a section containing 640 acres. Most farmers needed several sections in order to make a profitable living. Roads ran north and south, east and west, so it was not difficult to find one's way around the countryside.

We could look out our kitchen window for 100 miles to the west and there see the majestic Canadian Rockies. If you could be there and see the mountains in the various seasons of the year, you would agree with me that they were a sight to behold! One of the marvelous things about the mountains and the prairies was the mirages that spring out in the spring of the year.

I had heard of mirages, but I had never seen

one. Now here I was seeing them. In the spring the heat waves as they came in from the south to the north could be seen very clearly. They seemed to mysteriously change the landscape in a matter of seconds. Looking off into the distance one could see a building where there was no building, and as you looked the building would seem to grow taller, spring up into the air and seem to wobble, then drop back down to an almost invisible level. So it was with the mountains. As we looked, they would also assume various shapes. First they would just be a level range of black clouds, not a crack in the mountains; but as you gazed you would see gradually a small opening, then larger here, then there, until there were many cracks in the mountains. Then they would begin to deepen and seemingly grow tall, and still taller and taller into majestic steeples. Then they would level off and the process would be repeated over and over.

There was another miraculous thing that could be seen in the mountains. The winters were very cold; we saw the temperature drop to 50 and 60 degrees below zero. The snow would get very deep and the wind seemed to blow constantly. During these cold blasts, sometimes one could look to the west and see what was the beginning of one of the marvelous things to behold. It was called the chinook, the coming of the chinook winds. There was hanging over the mountains a great level cloud, a solid cloud. In between the cloud and the mountain there was a light, a very light colored space. One could prophesy what was coming. The chinook arch would form in this manner. The winds would begin to blow and no matter how cold it was, in the matter of a very short time the temperature would rise to well above zero. This would last perhaps as long as two or three days and then the cold would grip the countryside again and everything would be covered with snow and ice. People could skate for miles and miles.

At times such as this one could get snowbound, as the roads would be impassable or the "bottom would drop out" as the saying went, for when it thawed it was very muddy. It was difficult sometimes to get to the hospital or doctor which were 40 miles from where we lived. On occasion an airplane would have to be called to transport someone who was ill or had died.

Country Hospitality

I well remember one day my wife, Doris, made the trip to Calgary to the doctor, finding she needed to stay over night in order for tests to be completed. She checked out of the hotel where she had spent the night and went to the bus station, only to be told that the weather was so bad there would be no buses out until further notice. So she had to return to the hotel, and it was a full week before the roads could be traveled.

Most of the roads then were either gravel or dirt. During the summertime when it was very dry the roads would become quite dusty. I have seen it when there was no rain for many months. The dust would splash up on either side of the car almost like water. But watch out when there would be a dust storm! On one occasion I had been called to Calgary to conduct a funeral. I decided to take the closest route over some country roads. I ran into a dust storm and it would be hard for you to imagine the condition of my clothes. I had to go into a cleaning establishment and ask to have my suit cleaned before I could go to the service. So I went into a booth, took off my suit and waited until they gave it a quick cleaning. Then I proceeded to the funeral.

Another time, when I was exhausted at the close of a district meeting and hoped for a much needed bit of rest, suddenly the telephone rang and I heard the voice of the local elder telling me that he had a call to come to anoint an elderly lady who lived 125 miles to the north. This would mean a round trip of 250 miles.

We decided to take an extra day for the trip and visit other isolated members along the way. So you can readily see why the church newsletter was such a great help in keeping in touch with the church.

I am reminded of the time I went with the "executive secretary" who had come up from the States and another local board member to visit the inactive churches of Saskatchewan. Here were areas that had been settled earlier. Homes and churches had been built in what was then a thriving country. But as time passed the dry weather crept up on them, more and more each year until it was no longer profitable to continue farming in that section. Some folk moved farther north; others moved back to the States and the several churches that had been organized there became unused.

We traveled many, many miles to each point. I often wished I had a small plane or helicopter to use to get to those places, but of course never did realize this. The evening of the second day I had to leave the party and return home to perform a wedding. I went into the small station called

Rosedale, which I remember from some of the older radio plays. I had an Eastern Clergy Rail Permit, good only in the United States and especially in the eastern part of the U. S., or so I thought. I presented it and they honored it. I was buying a one-way ticket to Drumheller and the station attendant charged me half-fare. I boarded the train and spent the entire night traveling, reaching the next stop early in the morning. From here I had to take a bus on home, and again the clergy permit was honored by the bus clerk. Things like this were typical of most of the people in that great northern land.

There were many languages spoken in this section of Alberta. I was a member of the British and Foreign Bible Society and served on the board of directors which met monthly at Calgary in the Bible House. It was during these meetings that I learned that the scriptures were being published and circulated in Southern Alberta alone, in 47 different languages. I was fortunate that my work was among people for the most part who spoke English. Although I had studied both French and Latin, I could not speak either well enough to be effective.

I must relate yet another interesting experience while in this friendly land. I was attending a church conference in California and to my delight learned it was not too far from where our son, Ernest, was stationed. At the close of the conference I made plans to go to Oceanside, California, to visit Ernest and his wife for a short time. It was a happy reunion, I assure you.

On my way back home this incident happened. I was traveling by train through Vancouver, British Colombia, in a day coach. I had for a seat companion a Mexican-American, a short, stubby man, very friendly. When it came nighttime, he said, "Now I am going back to the smoking car and get some sleep. That will leave the entire seat for you to relax in." The next morning very early he rejoined me, after we both had had a good sleep. At the next stop we decided to walk out on the station platform and get some fresh air. Now during the night I had put my billfold inside my vest, thinking it would be safer than in my pocket, and I forgot to change it back the next morning.

I returned to my seat a little ahead of my new friend, and when he returned to his seat, he came up to me with a big grin and handed to me my billfold intact. He commented, "You must have dropped this on the platform. I am sure it is yours." I was very grateful to him and was once again reminded there are so many honest people still around.

We were truly among a people who were most generous, loving and sharing. They made us, as well as any others that were away from "home," feel their homes were our home. No one was ever left alone during the various holidays when families usually get together. One of the homes always added extra boards in the table to include everyone. If one happened, while making calls, to get to a home near meal time, there was no fluster evident; they just moved over and set another plate and shared such as was already prepared.

A Baptistry Healing

It was in 1948 that I terminated my services as pastor to the churches in Canada with regrets on the part of both the people there and us. However, the winters were very severe, our son had been released from the Navy and returned to the east. My mother was all alone and not well. So it was decided I would transfer my place of work back to the eastern part of the United States.

Annual Conference was to be held in Colorado Springs, so we left in time to visit Yellowstone Park on our way back, and then on to the conference. There we occupied the honeymoon room in one of the local motels, at the foot of the Garden of the Gods.

For a short time I was pastor of the Maple Spring congregation including six preaching points, in the First District of West Virginia. My wife as well as several other ministers in the congregation helped with the preaching.

Next we took a summer out to build my mother a small cottage in Buckhannon, W. Va., where she would be more comfortably located. That summer passed quickly with my mother settled in her new home and I was ready for the next assignment in Pocahontas County. We located at

Durbin where the church was not entirely finished. We had instructions to work toward the completion of this church, and we also did considerable work in remodeling or repairs on several of the other churches in the congregation. Once again we were in a place where there were not six but *seven* preaching points.

I do not recall any time when a change was in the making that we did not have to decide between at least two calls. One wonders what may have been different had we chosen the other place. We enjoyed the work in the new area very much, as we always did wherever we were located. From the start we always waited for a call, and when it came we felt that it was a call from God to work in that field at that place, at that time, without exception.

One of the more enjoyable things about living at Durbin, was that it was midway between Buckhannon, where we had settled my mother, and Staunton, Va., where our son now lived. I could continue to keep an eye on my mother and we could have some fellowship with our son and his family. This pleasure had been denied us before, since we were always separated by too great a distance to visit back and forth. At last we could for a brief time enjoy them and the grandsons.

Many interesting experiences were ours during this ministry. One day a dear sister came to me and said, "A sheep came to our pasture and we have been unable to locate the owner. So we sold it and I'd like for the money to go toward some special project." We needed a pulpit stand for the Durbin church, so the money was spent for lumber from which I built a nice chancel furniture set.

The Durbin church had a baptistry in it, the only one in this section of the country. A young lady from another denomination became ill with polio and was in the hospital for a long time. Finally she was told she could come home if she had some means of taking exercise in water. So the baptistry came into use for her weekly exercises. The water was heated during the Sunday morning services since the church was heated at that time. Then she used it in the afternoon.

She came in on crutches and some months later the crutches had disappeared and she was well.

The Durbin church was completed and fully equipped. The dedication services were held August 10, 1952. Mission completed.

Six Wedding Rings

In 1962 a call came for us to go to the Winter Park, Florida, church. This would be the first charge with just one preaching point in it. Here I could give all my time to just one group of people. It also meant I now had served in the most northern district and the most southern district of my church in North America. This move was a very great challenge, since the congregation was in a state of confusion. The former pastor had on one Sunday announced his resignation and the next Sunday he was in another part of the city taking with him some 40 to 50 members to start another church.

It was a difficult job to bring together the remaining members and heal the wounds that had been made. The remaining members dug in, however, and we went forward with a strong program; the church grew not only in members, but spiritually. It was a joy to work in this church and district.

Some months after my arrival there, on one of my trips out in the city locating members, I was involved in an accident. It wrapped my car around a grapefruit tree, and pushed my head through the windshield. I received a scalp wound, a basel skull fracture, various other broken facial bones, cuts and bruises. I was taken by ambulance to the Florida Sanitorium Hospital operated by the Seventh Day Adventist Church. I wasn't expected to live, but I recovered in some weeks sufficient enough to resume my duties. It is impossible to express my gratitude for the quick response of the ambulance attendants and the excellent care of the doctors, nurses and all who had a part in my recovery.

The church wrapped their arms of love and concern about us. My car was totaled, they helped me secure another car and assisted in many other ways both while I was in the hospital and during my recovery. The following summer I was given a leave of absence for three months to more fully recover from my injuries. I can say truthfully I do not remember a really well day since that time.

It was at Winter Park that I performed a triple wedding. The three Chambers sisters married in a single service. A special ceremony had to be written. To say the least, it was a bit tricky to handle six wedding rings in one service, but it went off beautifully.

Home Sweet Home

In the fall of 1955 we answered a call to the Martinsburg, W. Va., church which was then a part of the Middle Maryland District. This move would bring us closer to my mother, who had become very ill, and our son and family. My mother died a few months later and our son moved west the following summer. Once again we were separated from those dearest to us.

Home Sweet Home

> Today I wandered back again
> Into a woodland dell,
> And paused upon a little spot
> That once I knew so well,
> Where once a little cabin stood
> Midst strong and towering tree;
> It was the house my father built
> And home sweet home to me.
>
> But that was many years ago;
> The house is long since gone.
> And once again the tall trees grow
> Where was a grassy lawn.
> I gazed about with saddened heart,
> Some trace perchance to see

Of that love built with magic art—
A home sweet home for me.

I spoke aloud amidst the dell,
So silent and so still;
An answering voice I knew so well
Re-echoed from the hill.
And as I turned to wend my way
From that once homey scene,
I saw it snugly tucked away—
A spray of evergreen.

I stooped and touched it tenderly;
It seemed so meek and fair
I knew that mother years ago
In love had placed it there.
And once again in vision clear,
In memory glad and free,
I sensed that heavenly atmosphere
Of HOME SWEET HOME to me.

This church had two preaching points, Vanclesville, the parent church, and Martinsburg. This was a very active church with many opportunities in which to serve. Here again some remodeling and improvements were made in order to provide additional classrooms. A pastor's study was established at the church. Choir robes and new hymnals were added. A public address system was installed and an organ purchased.

Here there had been a divided faction. Again we were to be an instrument in helping to bind up old wounds so they could heal, and the church went forward with a Spirit-filled dedication.

Four years passed quickly and I felt that at my age and state of health, perhaps I would not be able to continue in the active pastoral work too many more years and should be thinking more seriously of retiring. So when a call came from the Buena Vista, Va., church we accepted, and made the move in the fall of 1959.

This move would bring us closer to a little cottage near Stuarts Draft that we had been working on for several years during vacations. From Buena Vista, we could go to work on it more often when we had a day off. We had taken our first meal at Martinsburg, with the Guy Kaylors, and in that home we had the last meal before leaving that community. Indeed one not only leaves a part of themselves but takes a part of those left behind with them with each move or separation. This was true at Martinsburg as well as in all other moves we had made.

Preparing the Way

We served the Buena Vista, Va., church for the next three years. It was a joy to work with the people there, not only the membership but the entire community. Both this church and the Martinsburg church were built with cut stone and were somewhat similar in design. The regular Sunday morning attendance filled the sanctuary to capacity, and every nook and corner was used for Sunday school classes. The seed was planted for an addition to the present building or a separate educational building. This seed grew and the dream was realized some years later.

We were the first minister-family to live in the lovely large parsonage that was under construction when we moved there. This seemed a good conclusion to my active full-time pastoral work. To be sure, it represented a big change in living accomodations from the tent that was our first "parsonage," but we would not have wanted to miss the experience of either one.

As time went on it became a reality that my full-time active pastoral ministry was drawing to a close due to health problems. So at the end of my third year I resigned, much to my regret, as it had been a very satisfying pastorate and a difficult decision to make. It would mean that now I would no longer be in the main stream of the church program. This I have missed very much.

We moved to Stuarts Draft, Va., to the little cottage we had been building for just such a time as this. It was not entirely ready for occupancy, and true to form the men of Buena Vista pitched in and helped build a garage and other things that needed to be done on the house before our moving. This was another second mile for them, as they had so many, many times taken charge and kept the work going during the times I was ill and in the hospital.

We spent the next five years there in our cottage and attended the Mt. Vernon church. For the first time I had a pastor and was on the outside looking in. This I enjoyed very much even though I missed to the end of my life the hustle-bustle of the pastoral ministry.

I soon learned that when one retires it does not mean he stops work! Activities at Mt. Vernon included teaching a class, going out to other churches for special services, and serving one summer as an interim pastor. I also served the Arcadia, Florida, church for almost two years during 1964-65 and then again in 1968-69.

If I was asked to sum up my ministry of 54 years I think I would have to say it could be divided into four periods. One, the free ministry, which included the years spent in school; two, home missions; three, self-supporting churches;

and four, after-retirement volunteer work.

Isaiah 6:8 was directed right to me: "Whom shall I send, and who will go for us? Then said I, Here am I; send me." And 40:30: "Prepare ye the way of the Lord, make straight in the desert a highway for our God."

The Last Move

We had a dream of some day returning to the Bridgewater, Va., community where we might be more conveniently located as well as be near a college which provided so many advantages in the cultural arts. So when the opportunity presented itself, we sold our cottage at Stuarts Draft and purchased a house on Broad Street in Bridgewater the fall of 1967. It was to be our last move.

We had a feeling of coming home. The church and community quickly wrapped their arms of welcome and love about us. I was asked to teach the Friendship Class, which I continued doing until illness confined me to home. The members of this class became very dear to me and I considered them an extension of my own family. Doris and I both became very involved in volunteer work at the home for the aging which is located nearby, also in many other activities in the community.

Here on September 5, 1971, we celebrated our 50th wedding anniversary with friends and relatives.

Sunset Days

June 25, 1973, the phone rang late at night . . . the tragic message—our son, Ernest, had died suddenly from a heart attack. He had been employed with the Philco-Ford Corporation for the past 17 years and was located at the Vandenburg Air Force Base, living in the nearby city of Lompoc, California. This was a blow that only those who have gone through it can understand—the grief and sorrow in losing a son and only child.

Sands of Time

I've read about the "sands of time"
And all the footprints there,
And as I muse, the heights sublime,
Above a world of care,
Shine forth in splendor, and with grace
Amongst God's works of art,
For footprints small are traced across
The tablet of my heart.

It seems that only yesterday
These little prints were made;
Still they are fresh in memory,
I know they will not fade.
I hear them yet as in a dream

Go toddling o'er the floor;
I see the dirty fingerprints
Upon the kitchen door.

The little face all smeared with jam
And lighted up with glee,
Those eyes abrim with wonderment
A-looking up at me,
The gentle clasp of little hands
A-holding on to mine,
The flights we took to Fairy Land
Are memories divine.

The tears must flow—I cannot keep
Them in their hidden beds;
I dream when I am fast asleep,
I see those tousled heads;
And should I own the universe,
Yea, all the wealth of man,
I'd give it all to have my dreams
Come back to life again.

We flew out to attend the funeral, and stayed with the family for several weeks. We are proud of Ernest and the record he left behind. The two grandsons, Richard and Robert, and Ernest's wife, Doris, continue to live in Lompoc. Now there are two great-grandsons, Marc and Michael, which I will not be privileged to ever see.* I love them all very much.

Vesper Thoughts

I saw the sun go down tonight
Beyond the western hills;
And as it passed beyond my sight,
So softly and so still,
I wondered if the happy hearts
Or those laid low by pain
Would, with the passing of the night
See it arise again.

I saw the golden sun tonight
Sink 'neath a threatening cloud;
And yet the sky above was bright—
Only a veiling shroud
Was cast about the distant hills
That darkened with the night.
I knew that in those distant rills
The sun was shining bright.

When I have seen the golden sun
Sink for the last for me,
And all my tasks of life are done,
And I put out to sea,
I only ask that I may gaze
Beyond the gathering night,
And see despite the twilight maze
God's love sun shining bright.

*The author, Robert, died March 2, 1975, four months after the taping of the contents of this book.

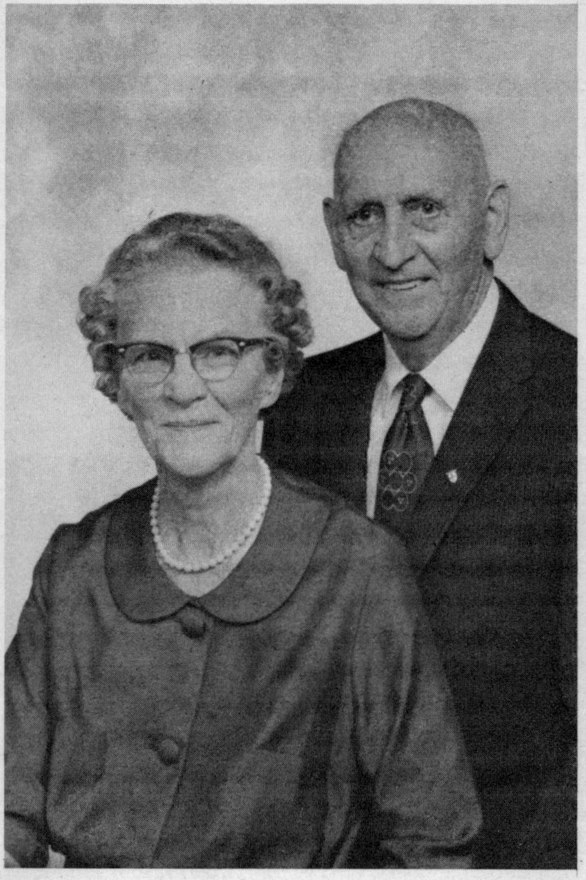

FUNDERBURG LIBRARY
MANCHESTER COLLEGE

DATE DUE

WITHDRAWN
from
Funderburg Library